Introduction

Welcome to "The Million Dollar Business". My name is Joshua Baumert and I want to take you on a journey – my journey from a simple client advisor in a small town to a successful entrepreneur with multiple sources of income. Are you ready to write your own story? Let's discover together how you can achieve financial freedom. Growing up in Beckum, North Rhine-Westphalia (Germany), my professional journey in the insurance industry began. But my dream was always to make more of my life and to be independent. What about you? Do you also have this inner urge to achieve something great? In this book, I share my ups and downs, the lessons I've learned, and the strategies that have helped me. My goal is to inspire you and give you the knowledge you need to find your own way. Let's get started together!

Chapter 1: How It All Began

Growing up in Beckum, a small town in North Rhine-Westphalia (Germany), my journey began with normal dreams and goals. Beckum, a city with just under 37,000 inhabitants, offered an idyllic backdrop for my childhood and youth. The close-knit community, traditions and family atmosphere shaped my early years. My parents gave me values such as honesty, diligence and perseverance at an early age.

Beckum was not just a city, but a safe haven where I experienced many unforgettable moments. I remember the Sunday walks with my family through the city park, the bike rides through the surrounding fields and the festivals that regularly took place on the market square. The close connection of the residents and the feeling of belonging gave me a solid basis for my later life.

After graduating from secondary school and graduating from high school, I originally wanted to join the police. It was not only the desire for a secure profession, but also the urge to serve my community and ensure justice. But fate had other plans. I had missed the entrance exam by one point. The disappointment was enormous. It was as if a part of my identity was suddenly questioned. But I thought early on that if anything happens, it doesn't happen for no reason. Perhaps in retrospect it was a good thing, because in this day and age it has probably become more and more dangerous. That's why I would like to take this opportunity to show my utmost respect and gratitude to the police.

My plan was to somehow bridge the time so that I could try again next time. A reasonable education was definitely needed. Later, I can always try my luck with the police, I thought to myself. So I decided to do a commercial apprenticeship at a large insurance company. That was definitely a good decision, because here I also learned a lot of things that were important for my future. Dealing with money, which insurances you really need and how the whole commercial topic actually works – all this was new and fascinating to me. In any case, I learned a lot during this time, which has helped me a lot in my current situation as an entrepreneur. I would definitely say that a sound education is the key and very important for your professional career. Because here I learned what was not actually taught at school. A drastic experience was the day I looked after my first own customer. It was an elderly couple who were worried about their retirement provision. Through my knowledge and advice, I was able to help them put their finances in order and give them a sense of security. This feeling of being able to really make a difference was priceless and strengthened my decision.

One thing was clear: I was never a high-flyer at school. I always thought to myself, what do I need this for? I never have to analyze poems, pull the root out of anything or jump over a pole in the Fosbury flop. Do you know the feeling when the bar slips off and you fall with your back on this stupid bar? Oh man, I could write a lot more about it, but I think I would have to mention all of this in a sequel.

I was never a teacher's favorite either. Even then, it was sometimes noticeable that I had a little stubborn head from time to time and didn't like to be told anything. You noticed that later in my salaried jobs. I was simply not born to let others dictate to me or even to work for others. I always wanted to do "my own thing".

My parents didn't always think this was appropriate, and it often ended in discussions. When I look back on it, however, all this was only well-intentioned, because they always wanted only the best for me. But now back to my education, which was certainly also due to some pressure from my parents, which is why I am very grateful to them. My mother, a warm-hearted woman with a sharp mind, and my father, an extremely hardworking man, attached great importance to my receiving a solid education. They saw in me the potential that I didn't quite recognize at that time.

It was definitely a very big milestone for me, as I finally realized that it brought me something in my life. Early on, I learned the importance of hard work and perseverance. My first professional experience as a client advisor helped me develop valuable skills that would be invaluable later in my career. During this time, I realized that I wanted more than just a secure job – I wanted financial independence and the freedom to create my own life.

This was also the reason why I started to educate myself with various books about mindset, real estate, entrepreneurship, personal development and wealth accumulation. And I can absolutely recommend that to you. If you find yourself here as well, I definitely advise you to start reading. In any case, that has had a significant impact on my success. Among other things, I can recommend the book "Rich Dad, Poor Dad" by Robert T. Kiyosaki or "Richer than the Geissens" by Alex Düsseldorf Fischer. For more recommendations or tips, feel free to write to me via Instagram. I am always very happy to receive messages and am happy to answer any questions or suggestions you may have.

In Beckum, I was surrounded by people who had their own stories and challenges. It was a city where everyone knew everyone else and where people could rely on each other. Knowing that you were part of such a close-knit community often gave me strength and support, especially in times of doubt and uncertainty.

During my apprenticeship at the insurance company, I was surrounded by colleagues who inspired and motivated me. Some of them had already had impressive careers and were happy to share their experiences and advice with me. These mentors helped me refine my skills and prepare me for the challenges of the business world. They showed me the importance of building a network and learning from the experiences of others.

A particular challenge during my training was dealing with difficult customers. There were days when I felt like nothing was going right and every customer was unhappy. But over time, I learned to be patient and respond to the needs of the customers. These experiences taught me valuable lessons in communication and conflict resolution that would serve me well in my later career.

Parallel to my professional development, I began to deal more intensively with personal development. I read books and attended seminars that helped me strengthen my mindset and define my goals more clearly. One book that had a big impact on me was "Rich Dad, Poor Dad" by Robert T. Kiyosaki. It opened my eyes to the opportunities that financial education and smart investments can offer. This book was the trigger for my interest in real estate and wealth accumulation.

Another book that changed my way of thinking was *Richer than the Geissens* by Alex Düsseldorf Fischer. It gave me valuable insights into the world of entrepreneurship and motivated me to go my own way. These books were not only sources of inspiration, but also practical guides that helped me take concrete steps towards achieving my goals.

During this time, I also began to work on my physical fitness. Sport became an important part of my life and helped me to reduce stress and boost my self-confidence. I joined a local gym and started working out regularly. The discipline and perseverance I gained from training carried over to other areas of my life, helping me stay focused and motivated.

One of the most valuable lessons I learned at this stage of my life was the importance of resilience. There were a lot of setbacks and challenges, but I learned that it's not about how many times you fall, but how often you get back up. This attitude helped me to keep going despite the disappointments and obstacles and not to lose sight of my goals.

My parents continued to play an important role in my life. They supported me unconditionally and encouraged me to go my own way. Their love and support gave me the strength to persevere even in difficult times. Especially my mother, who always had an open ear for my worries and fears, was an invaluable source of support.

My friends were also an important support. We spent many evenings talking about our dreams and goals and motivating each other. These conversations were often a welcome balance to the challenges of everyday life and helped me to maintain my perspective.

During my training, I also learned the importance of hard work and perseverance. My first professional experience as a client advisor helped me develop valuable skills that would be invaluable later in my career. I realized that success doesn't come overnight, but is the result of continuous effort and dedication.

A particularly formative moment in my training was the first time I was able to help a client cope with a difficult financial situation. It was an elderly couple who had gotten into financial difficulties due to wrong investments. Thanks to my advice and support, they were able to get their finances back under control and secure their retirement provision. This experience not only gave me job satisfaction, but also the feeling that I could really make a difference in people's lives.

The journey, which began with normal dreams and goals, developed into a path full of challenges, setbacks and triumphs. Beckum, the small town in North Rhine-Westphalia, was the starting point of my journey, which made me what I am today. The values and lessons I learned there formed the basis for my further path and helped me overcome life's obstacles.

The decision to educate myself with books on mindset, real estate, entrepreneurship, personal development and wealth accumulation was a decisive step on my way to financial independence and personal freedom. These books not only gave me the necessary knowledge, but also the inspiration and motivation to pursue my dreams and not give up.

If you find yourself here as well, I definitely advise you to start reading. In any case, that has had a significant impact on my success. Among other things, I can recommend the book "Rich Dad, Poor Dad" by Robert T. Kiyosaki or "Richer than the Geissens" by Alex Düsseldorf Fischer. For more recommendations or tips, feel free to write to me via Instagram. I am always very happy to receive messages and am happy to answer any questions or suggestions you may have.

Growing up in Beckum and shaped by the experiences and challenges of my youth, I am now an entrepreneur who pursues his dreams and encourages others to do the same. The journey wasn't always easy, but it taught me that it's worth fighting for your goals and never giving up. The first steps may have been modest, but they have laid the foundation for an exciting and fulfilling journey that is far from over.

Chapter 2: The World of Insurance

Working as a customer advisor in the insurance industry was instructive, but not what I imagined in the long term. The desire for more financial freedom and independence grew steadily in me. But before I took this step, I gained valuable experience in dealing with customers and learned the art of sales, which gave me deep insights into human needs and behaviors.

The insurance industry provided me with a solid foundation and taught me important principles of finance. I learned how to assess risk, sell products and build long-term customer relationships. These skills formed the foundation for my future entrepreneurial activities. It was a time when I learned a lot about the importance of trust and reliability. Every conversation with a client was a way to sharpen my skills and develop a better understanding of people's financial needs.

But despite all the stability and security, I felt that this was not the path that really fulfilled me. I really enjoyed customer contact and sales, and I noticed that I could earn really good money here. But the problem as an employee was that I always earned the same, regardless of my performance. I had my goals, but when I exceeded them – which was often the case – I got at most a wet handshake. But woe betide me, I was once under it. After all, that could happen sometimes: vacation, illness, etc. I hadn't imagined it that way. If you sell a lot, you should get more for it than those who just about achieve their goals.

This dissatisfaction did not let me go. There had to be something where this was possible. So I started looking and researched intensively. I read books, browsed the Internet and talked to people who had already taken the path to self-employment. Every small success and every realization strengthened my desire to build something of my own.

During this time, I began to doubt my own potential and often wondered if I had the courage to leave the safe haven and set off into the unknown. But with each passing day, I realized that I would never be truly happy if I continued to rely only on the security of a steady job. I wanted to write my own story, be independent, and have full control over my income and time.

The transition from a secure job to something of my own was scary and exciting at the same time. I knew I would run into risks, but I was willing to take those risks to realize my vision of financial freedom and self-determination. The insurance industry had given me the tools I needed, but it was time to use those tools in a new, exciting way.

This inner drive led me to leave my comfort zone and take the first steps towards self-employment. I knew this was the beginning of a new journey – a journey that would challenge me and make me grow. And so I began to leave the world of insurance behind and find my own path, a path that would lead me to the financial freedom and independence I so desperately desired.

Insight into the world of insurance consulting

My years as a customer advisor in the insurance industry were marked by a wide range of experiences and encounters. Every day was a new challenge, whether it was selling complex insurance products or servicing long-standing customers. One particular moment that I remember was advising a family whose house was damaged by a severe storm. They were frightened and unsure how they could rebuild their livelihoods. It was in moments like these that I realized how important my work was—not just as a salesperson, but as someone who could help people in difficult life situations.

The insurance industry taught me to look at risk from different perspectives. Each insurance product had its specific terms and exclusions that needed to be understood. For many people, insurance is a complex topic full of uncertainties and misunderstandings. As a consultant, it was my job to make this complexity understandable and to offer tailor-made solutions.

The Art of Sales and Customer Relationship Management

Another essential aspect of my job was the sale of insurance products. It was not just selling a product, but understanding the needs and concerns of customers and offering the right solution based on that. Every customer was different: some were cautious and took a lot of time to build trust, while others were quick to make a decision. Flexibility and empathy were therefore essential to be successful.

Building long-term customer relationships was also of great importance. A satisfied customer was not just a one-time deal, but potentially a long-term partner. I learned how important it is to gain trust and maintain a good relationship at eye level. Looking back, I can say that these skills – the art of sales and customer relationship management – have served me not only in my time as a consultant, but also as a valuable foundation for my self-employment.

Limits of Security: The Desire for More

Despite the challenges and successes in my job as a customer advisor, I felt an increasing dissatisfaction. It was not only the monotonous security of a fixed salary that bothered me, but also the limited opportunities to increase my income through my performance. As an employee, my earnings were tied to fixed salary structures that offered little room for personal initiative and financial appreciation.

These restrictions led me to long for more independence and self-determination. I no longer wanted to be just a cog in the system, but to set my own goals and take full responsibility for my actions. The idea of using my skills and knowledge in an entrepreneurial context became more and more attractive.

The turning point: the decision to become self-employed

The transition from a secure job to something of his own was a process that did not come overnight. It was a step-by-step process of thinking, researching and planning. Every day brought new insights and insights that strengthened my decision. I began to analyze my financial possibilities and develop a plan on how to realize my vision of financial freedom and independence.

The turning point came when I admitted to myself that I was willing to give up the security of my job to start my own business. It was a decision that was marked by courage and determination – the decision to leave my comfort zone and take the leap into the unknown. I was willing to take risks and take on challenges to make my dream come true.

The importance of self-reflection and personal growth

In the months before my decision to become self-employed, I reflected intensively on my strengths and weaknesses. I analyzed what skills I needed to develop and what resources I had at my disposal. Self-reflection became an important tool to clearly define my goals and create a clear roadmap for the future.

This period of self-reflection was also a time of personal growth. I had to learn to overcome my fears and doubts and believe in myself. It was a journey of self-discovery that empowered me to make bold decisions and take responsibility for my own happiness.

The beginning of a new journey

The day I handed in my resignation and had my last day as an employee marked the beginning of a new journey. It was a sense of freedom and excitement that filled me—the certainty that I had regained control of my life. I was ready to take on the challenges of self-employment and build my business.

The world of insurance had taught me valuable lessons that I could now apply in my own business. Knowledge of customer management, sales and risk assessment formed the foundation on which I built my entrepreneurial ambitions. I was determined to use these tools in a new, creative way and successfully run my own business.

Result

The chapter of my career in the insurance industry was not only a period of professional development, but also a time of personal transformation. It was the time when I defined my passions and ambitions more clearly and found the courage to go my own way. The decision to leave the world of employees behind and choose self-employment was a step I have never regretted.

In the coming chapters, I will dive deeper into my experience as an entrepreneur and describe the ups and downs of my journey to financial freedom and independence. Every turn, challenge, and success has shaped me and made me the entrepreneur I am today.

Chapter 3: The Leap into Self-Employment

One day the time had come. A conversation with a good acquaintance opened my horizons and was to change my life. We sat together with a beer in a cozy round and let the carnival evening come to an end. Beckum, my small hometown, may be small, but it's known for one thing – carnival. And we are really good at that. If you feel like it, feel free to take a look. It's really worth it, and who knows, maybe we'll meet there.

In any case, we sat together and exchanged ideas about our work, reported news and complained about our respective worries and frustrations. I also gave free rein to my frustration. "It can't be," I said, "that I get the same for more work as someone who barely achieves his goals." That's when my acquaintance told me about someone who is self-employed in the financial services industry. At the time, to be honest, I didn't really know what it meant to be self-employed. But the fact was, the way things were going at the moment, it couldn't go on. Something had to change.

Finally, I agreed and allowed him to pass on my number. This step, as inconspicuous as it seemed, would turn out to be the beginning of an exciting and challenging journey. Although this time was made more difficult by the Corona pandemic, it laid the foundation for my path to self-employment. Looking back, this phase was an important lesson in resilience and adaptability.

The challenges of self-employment

Self-employment brought many challenges. Suddenly, I was no longer only responsible for my work, but also for my own company. I had to learn how to run a business, develop marketing strategies, and make informed financial decisions. The pandemic made that time even more difficult, but it also strengthened my will and determination to succeed.

Every day in self-employment was a new challenge. It was a constant learning and adaptation. I had to acquire knowledge in areas that were completely foreign to me before. This included accounting, legal issues and, above all, marketing. How do I reach my target group? How do I build a brand? These questions occupied me day and night.

A particularly formative experience was the first major marketing campaign that I set up on my own. With a limited budget and not much experience, I had to be creative and find the right channels to promote my offer. The first successes were not long in coming and strengthened me in my project.

Another crucial point was networking. I quickly learned that relationships and contacts are invaluable in the business world. Each new acquaintance brought new opportunities and perspectives. I participated in numerous online seminars and networking events to expand my knowledge and make valuable connections.

The pandemic as a challenge and an opportunity

The Covid-19 pandemic posed a particularly big challenge. Suddenly, face-to-face contact was severely limited, and many traditional business models had to be reconsidered. However, instead of getting discouraged, I saw this as an opportunity to improve my digital skills and find new ways to offer my services. Virtual meetings, online consulting and social media became my most important tools.

This time also taught me the importance of being flexible and adapting quickly to new situations. The ability to find creative solutions under pressure became one of my greatest strengths. Looking back, I am grateful for these challenges, because they made me the entrepreneur I am today.
The beginning of a new journey

The day I handed in my resignation and had my last day as an employee marked the beginning of a new journey. It was a sense of freedom and excitement that filled me—the certainty that I had regained control of my life. I was ready to take on the challenges of self-employment and build my business.

The world of insurance had taught me valuable lessons that I could now apply in my own business. Knowledge of customer management, sales and risk assessment formed the foundation on which I built my entrepreneurial ambitions. I was determined to use these tools in a new, creative way and successfully run my own business.

Result

The chapter of my career in the insurance industry was not only a period of professional development, but also a time of personal transformation. It was the time when I defined my passions and ambitions more clearly and found the courage to go my own way. The decision to leave the world of the employee behind me and decide to become self-employed was a step I have never regretted.

In the coming chapters, I will dive deeper into my experience as an entrepreneur and describe the ups and downs of my journey to financial freedom and independence. Every turn, challenge, and success has shaped me and made me the entrepreneur I am today.

If you also feel the urge to do more with your life and go your own way, then I encourage you to take the step. It won't always be easy, but it will be worth it. Stay curious, constantly learn and be willing to take risks. Your success begins where your comfort zone ends.

Chapter 4: Setbacks and New Beginnings

After the end of my cooperation with the financial service provider, I was faced with the question of what to do next. Various white-collar jobs didn't fulfill me, and I quickly realized that I wanted more. Books, YouTube videos, and education helped me plan my next move. I knew that I wanted to build something. Your own business, your own business idea, added value. Something that no one can take away from me. I wanted to create something big that I could pass on to my children one day.

I already knew the Geissens and their history and beginnings in the fashion industry from previous series. They were a kind of role model for me. Her attitude to life fascinated me. Even though they may have had to struggle with many prejudices, I always looked "behind the scenes" and found it impressive what they had built up. That's exactly what is important: You need someone you see as a role model and who you can look up to in difficult times. I always thought to myself: If others can do it, why can't I?

In this phase, I learned the importance of personal development and self-motivation. I devoured books on entrepreneurship, finance, and personal development. YouTube videos and online courses expanded my knowledge and helped me gain new perspectives. This time was characterized by self-reflection and the search for the right path. It was not only a professional, but also a personal transformation.

One of the books that particularly inspired me was "Rich Dad, Poor Dad" by Robert T. Kiyosaki. It opened my eyes to the possibilities of financial education and the importance of wealth accumulation. Another book that had a big influence on me was "Richer than the Geissens" by Alex Fischer. These works showed me that financial freedom and entrepreneurial success are achievable if you are willing to work hard and make smart decisions.

In addition to reading, I began to delve deeper into online educational resources. YouTube became my university. Channels of successful entrepreneurs, financial experts and motivational speakers offered me valuable insights and practical tips. I learned how to plan a business, develop marketing strategies and make financial decisions. The stories of people who had managed to become successful despite great adversity were particularly helpful. These stories gave me hope and motivation.
A pivotal moment was when I signed up for my first online course. It was a course on digital marketing, and it helped me understand the basics of online business. I learned the importance of a strong online presence and how to attract customers through targeted marketing. These skills were crucial in building my own business.

Personal training and self-motivation were not always easy. There were days when I doubted my abilities and wondered if I had taken the right path. However, every time I read a new book or watched an inspirational video, my faith in myself was strengthened. I realized that the key to success is to never give up and to constantly strive for knowledge and improvement.

During this time, I also began to develop my own ideas for a business. I wanted to create something that would add real value while leveraging my passions and skills. I thought about what problems I could solve and how I could help people achieve their goals. This process of brainstorming was exciting and scary at the same time, but it was also the beginning of a new, exciting journey.

The challenges of implementation

Turning my ideas into reality was no less challenging. The transition from planning to concrete implementation required courage, determination and a clear strategy. I had to learn how to turn a vision into a tangible business that offers real value and is sustainable.

A significant setback on my path was the financial aspect. As a budding entrepreneur, I was prepared for financial challenges to arise, but the reality still proved to be more challenging than expected. Raising start-up capital and ensuring a stable cash flow were key challenges that I had to deal with intensively.

The first few months of my business were marked by uncertainty. There were times when I doubted the future of my company and felt the temptation to give up. But every time these thoughts came up, I remembered my motivation and the vision that had driven me to take this path.

The importance of the network

Another key factor in my success was networking. I learned that relationships and contacts are invaluable in the business world. I participated in industry events, made contacts with other entrepreneurs and subject matter experts, and continuously expanded my network. These connections not only brought new business opportunities, but also valuable support and advice during difficult times.

The importance of resilience and perseverance

The biggest lesson I've taken away from this stage of my life is the importance of resilience and perseverance. Every setback and challenge has been an opportunity for growth and personal development. I learned to accept my mistakes as part of the learning process and to learn from them.

Result

Looking back, the phase of setbacks and new beginnings was one of the most formative and instructive times of my life. It has had a strong impact on me not only professionally, but also personally and helped me grow as an entrepreneur. The skills, knowledge and experience I gained during this time form the foundation of my success today.

If you find yourself in a similar situation and are thinking about going your own way, I encourage you to be brave and follow your dreams. The path may not always be easy, but it will be worth it. Don't let setbacks discourage you, but see them as part of your growth process. Stay focused, constantly learn, and be ready to take on the challenges that lie ahead. Your success is in your hands.

Chapter 5: The Path to Your Own Online Business

The idea of an online business that generates passive income has fascinated me for a long time. After my experience of self-employment in the financial services industry, I was hungry for a new challenge. The start, however, was rocky and full of uncertainties. But I finally knew exactly what I wanted to build: my hobby should become a profession, and so I decided to start my own fitness clothing brand. The process was challenging, but also incredibly exciting. From the creation of the online shop to the selection of products and marketing – I put my heart and soul into this project.

The beginning of the online store

When the shop finally went online, the tension was almost unbearable. Anyone who has ever set up their own online shop knows this indescribable feeling when the first order arrives. I still remember the name of the first customer exactly. It was a moment of deep satisfaction and pride. This moment confirmed to me that I was on the right path, even though I knew that the path was far from over.

At first, I kept my plans mostly to myself. Only my family and my girlfriend knew about it, because my girlfriend was of course very supportive of me here as well. Your support was and is invaluable to me. Without them, many things would certainly have been more difficult. But of course my plan did not go completely unnoticed. My employer, who employed me at the time, had to learn about my plans because it was important to maintain transparency.

The decision for your own business

When my employer at the bank found out about my new project, he presented me with a tough decision: bank or business. It was one of the hardest decisions of my life, but I knew that my heart beat for my own business. So I put all my eggs in one basket and decided to pursue my dream. The thought of building my own company and turning my passion into a profession never left me.

The Challenges and Triumphs

Building my online business has been a journey full of challenges and triumphs. I learned how to create a website, market products, and attract customers. Every little hurdle I overcame strengthened my confidence in myself and my project. The first sales were a big milestone, but there were still many obstacles to overcome. Through hard work, determination, and continuous improvement, my business began to grow slowly but surely.

The first phase after launching an online store is crucial for success. Here are some valuable tips and lessons I've learned while building my fitness clothing brand:

1. Market analysis and target group determination

Before you even set up an online store, it's important to thoroughly analyze the market. What are the needs of your potential customers? Who is your target audience and what is the best way to reach them? A detailed market analysis will help you plan your product offering and marketing strategies in a targeted manner.

2. Selection of products and suppliers

The selection of products is a central point for the success of your online store. Make sure that your products appeal to a clear target group and stand out from the competition. In addition, cooperation with reliable suppliers is essential to ensure a smooth supply chain and ensure customer satisfaction.

3. Build a professional online presence

An appealing and user-friendly website is the be-all and end-all for your online store. Invest in a professional design that reflects your brand's aesthetic. A clear structure, easy navigation and meaningful product descriptions are crucial to convert visitors into customers.

4. Implement an effective marketing strategy

Without a well-thought-out marketing strategy, it's going to be hard to drive traffic to your website and generate sales. Use various channels such as social media, content marketing, search engine optimization (SEO), and paid advertising to increase your reach. Continuously test and optimize your marketing activities to increase effectiveness.

5. Customer loyalty and service quality

The satisfaction of your customers is crucial for the long-term success of your online business. Provide excellent customer service, respond to inquiries in a timely manner, and respond to feedback. Not only is a happy customer more likely, but they also become an ambassador for your brand and can attract new customers through positive word-of-mouth.

6. Financial planning and scalability

Always keep an eye on your financial expenses and plan for the long term. Set clear goals and track your performance regularly with the help of analytics tools. Scale your business in a controlled manner and invest in growth when the time comes. A solid financial basis is essential for long-term success.

The learning process and personal development

It was a time of intensive learning and personal development. I continued to devour books on entrepreneurship and marketing, watched countless YouTube videos, and took online courses to constantly expand my skills. One particularly valuable course was on digital marketing, which helped me understand and successfully apply the basics of online business. This new knowledge was crucial in building my own business.

But it wasn't just the knowledge that helped me move forward. It was also the passion and vision to create something of my own that offers real added value to myself and others. This vision kept me motivated to keep going even in difficult times. Looking back, each challenge was a valuable lesson that made me stronger and more experienced.

The role of support

My family, and especially my girlfriend, played a crucial role in my journey. They were not only emotional supporters, but also practical supporters in difficult phases. Her belief in me and my project gave me the strength to continue even in times of uncertainty. Their encouragement and understanding have been priceless and have always motivated me to be the best I can be.

The evolution of the brand

Over time, my fitness clothing brand became an established name in the industry. Through targeted marketing, social media presence and customer feedback, I was able to continuously expand the brand and expand the range. Every step forward has been a success, due to hard work and the support of my team.

The balance between work and life

Balancing my online business and my personal life has been a constant challenge. As an entrepreneur, I was often busy around the clock, and it took discipline and organization to balance these two areas. I learned to prioritize and develop efficient work habits to succeed both professionally and personally.

The Importance of Failure

Not every step on my path was crowned with success. There were times when marketing campaigns didn't bring the desired success or product decisions had to be reconsidered. But I learned to learn from these moments of failure and to emerge stronger from them. Every failure was a chance to rethink my strategies and develop my skills.

The future of the company

Today I look back proudly on the path I have taken. My online business is not only a successful business, but also a symbol of the realization of my dreams. It shows that with hard work, passion and the right support, almost anything is possible. If you find yourself in a similar situation and are thinking about going your own way, I encourage you to be brave and believe in your dreams. The journey may be difficult, but the reward is well worth it.

Final Thoughts

The decision to start my own online business was one of the best decisions of my life. She has not only advanced me professionally, but also developed me as a person. I have learned that success does not come overnight, but is the result of perseverance, passion and the courage to follow your dreams. If you feel the desire to build something of your own, be ready for the challenges, but also be confident that each step will bring you closer to your goals.

Chapter 6: The Power of Marketing

Marketing is at the heart of any successful business. It's the tool that makes your business visible and attracts customers. In this chapter, I share the most valuable tips and tricks that have helped me take my business to the next level.

At the beginning of my marketing journey

When I was intensively involved in marketing for my online business, I was overwhelmed by the numerous possibilities and strategies. But I quickly realized that a strong online presence and targeted advertising campaigns would be crucial to my success. From social media to content marketing to search engine optimization, I discovered the many ways to promote my business.

Social Media: The Power of Networks

Social media is indispensable for every business today. Platforms like Instagram, Facebook, and TikTok offer the opportunity to interact directly with the target audience and build a loyal community. Through regular posts, interactive stories and targeted advertisements, I was able to significantly increase the reach of my company. It was especially important to stay authentic and share content that reflected my passion and vision.

Instagram as a central platform

Instagram proved to be particularly effective in building my brand. Through visually appealing posts and stories, I was not only able to capture the attention of my target group, but also build a strong community. The key was to share content that represented not only my products, but also a lifestyle that my customers appreciated.

Facebook for targeted ads

On Facebook, I used targeted ads to attract new customers and strengthen existing customer loyalty. The wide range of targeting options allowed me to run ads based on demographics, interests, and behaviors of my target audience. This helped me use my marketing budgets efficiently and maximize the ROI of my campaigns.

TikTok as an emerging platform

TikTok was an up-and-coming platform that I used for viral marketing. Through creative and entertaining content, I was able to appeal to a younger audience and quickly increase awareness of my brand. The use of hashtags and trends allowed me to generate organic reach and further drive my branding.

Content Marketing: Providing Added Value

Content marketing was another important pillar of my strategy. By creating blog posts, videos, and tutorials, I was able to provide real value to my clients while also demonstrating my expertise in the fitness industry. Not only did this help build trust, but it also helped to better position my website in search engines.

Blog posts as a source of information

Creating regular blog posts on relevant topics in the fitness industry helped me inform my target audience and drive traffic to my website in the long run. SEO-optimized articles improved the visibility of my content in search engine results and attracted organic traffic that turned into qualified leads.

Engagement videos and tutorials

Creating videos and tutorials allowed me to show my products in action and demonstrate my expertise. YouTube and other video platforms offered an ideal way to explain complex topics in a simple way while strengthening my brand. Customers appreciated the hands-on guides and recommended my videos to others, resulting in an organic growth rate.

Search Engine Optimization (SEO): Increase Visibility

SEO is a complex but incredibly effective tool. I invested a lot of time and effort to understand and apply the basics of search engine optimization. By optimizing my website and content, I was able to ensure that my online shop was found better in the search results of Google and Co. This led to more organic traffic and ultimately more sales.

Keyword research and on-page optimization

Conducting thorough keyword research helped me identify relevant search terms that my target audience was using. Integrating these keywords into my product pages, blog posts, and meta descriptions improved my pages' rankings and attracted qualified traffic. On-page optimizations such as fast loading times, mobile optimization, and user-friendly navigation also helped improve user experience and search engine rankings.

Backlink Building and Off-Page SEO

Building high-quality backlinks from trusted websites increased my website's authority in the eyes of search engines like Google. Through targeted off-page SEO, I was able to expand the reach of my content and generate additional traffic through external links. The focus was on building natural and relevant backlinks that added to my brand's credibility.

Targeted advertising campaigns: maximise efficiency

One of the biggest challenges was to create low-cost and profitable advertising campaigns. In the beginning, I had worked with various agencies, but the results often fell short of my expectations. Finally, I decided to take the wheel into my own hands and acquire the necessary knowledge. By continuously learning and adapting my strategies, I was finally able to run efficient advertising campaigns that reached my target audience exactly where they were.

Paid Search Advertising

With paid search ads, I was able to target people who were actively searching for my products. By selecting relevant keywords and optimizing my ad copy, I managed to maximize the click-through rate and generate qualified leads. Analyzing campaign data and continuously optimizing helped me use the budget efficiently and increase the ROI of my PPC campaigns.

Social Media Advertising

On platforms like Facebook and Instagram, I used targeted ads to reach my target audience and increase brand awareness. Selecting demographics, interests, and behaviors allowed me to tailor my ads to the needs and preferences of my potential customers. A/B testing and campaign performance analysis helped me optimize the effectiveness of my social media advertising and reduce the cost per click.

Learning and adapting: The key to success

Marketing is not a static process. It requires constant learning and adapting to new trends and technologies. I read countless books, watched webinars and took online courses to stay up to date. Courses on digital marketing, conversion optimization, and marketing analysis were particularly helpful, helping me to further refine my strategies and maximize my successes.

Progress through analysis and measurement

Regularly analyzing marketing data was crucial to my strategic decision-making. By using analytics tools like Google Analytics, I was able to accurately track user behavior on my website and gain insights that helped optimize my campaigns. Measuring metrics like conversion rates, clicks, and customer acquisition costs helped me make informed decisions and use my marketing budgets efficiently.

Agile Marketing Approaches

Agile methods such as A/B testing and iterative campaign optimization helped me to react quickly to changes in the market and continuously improve my marketing strategies. By testing different ad variants, target group targets, and ad formats, I was able to find out which approaches worked best and achieved the greatest return on investment. The flexibility and adaptability of these approaches allowed me to make my marketing activities agile and stay on track for success.

Using your own knowledge: Staying independent

Although it can be tempting to outsource many marketing tasks to external experts, it was important for me to learn and implement as much as possible on my own. Of course, you can't know everything and sometimes experts are essential, but for many areas I wanted to stay in control and continuously expand my knowledge. This allowed me to ensure that my marketing strategies were always in line with my expectations and that I was able to make adjustments at any time.

Personal development and knowledge expansion

My personal development in marketing has been a continuous journey. I took every opportunity to expand my knowledge of new techniques, tools, and best practices. Engaging with other marketing experts and participating in industry events helped me gain new perspectives and continuously improve my skills. By sharing insights and experiences with like-minded people, I was able to benefit from their feedback and further deepen my expertise.

Conclusion: The essence of marketing

Marketing is an art and a science at the same time. It requires creativity, analytics and, above all, perseverance. The insights and experiences I gained along the way have been crucial to the success of my business. By continuously developing and adapting my marketing strategies, I was able to take my business to the next level and build a loyal customer community. If you also have the dream of running a successful online business, I advise you to deal intensively with marketing. It will be worth it – I promise you.

The importance of a clear vision

A clear vision and a deep understanding of your target audience are the cornerstones of any successful marketing strategy. Invest time and energy in defining your brand values and positioning. Understand your customers' needs and pain points and develop solutions that add real value. By focusing your marketing efforts on meeting these needs and communicating your message clearly, you can build long-term relationships and position your brand successfully.

Continuous innovation and adaptation

The market and technologies are constantly evolving, so it's crucial that you remain flexible and continuously adapt your marketing strategies. Be willing to explore new channels, try innovative approaches, and respond to feedback. Use analytics tools and data to make informed decisions and use your marketing investments efficiently. By continuously educating yourself and sharpening your skills, you can ensure that your marketing efforts are successful in the long run.

The role of authenticity and transparency

Authenticity is a crucial factor in building trust and long-term customer relationships. Be honest and transparent in your communication and avoid presenting a false identity or promises. Customers value honesty and openness, and are more willing to work with brands that share their values and provide authentic experiences. Maintain open communication with your community and be willing to listen to feedback and adjust your strategies accordingly.

Final Thoughts

The decision to start and successfully market my own online business was one of the most rewarding experiences of my life. By using effective marketing strategies, I was able to not only increase the visibility of my brand, but also build strong customer loyalty. Every entrepreneur who pursues his dream should deal intensively with marketing and take advantage of the many opportunities to advance his business. The journey may be challenging, but with passion, dedication and continuous improvement, success is within reach.

Chapter 7: The Path to Sustainable Prosperity

From a young age, I understood the importance of smart investments. This knowledge has helped me enormously on my way to financial independence. In this chapter, I would like to show you how to invest money wisely and invest it in your business in order to be successful in the long term. From the stock market to real estate, the right decisions can make all the difference. I was always fascinated by how large companies worked and how you could participate in their successes.

The basics of investing

Investing means making your money work for you instead of just saving it. The difference between saving and investing is crucial: while saving means setting aside money to use later, investing aims to increase the money you have. This can be done through various forms of investment, which are explained below.

Stocks and ETFs

One of the most well-known forms of investment is stocks. Buying shares means buying shares in a company. As the company grows and makes a profit, the value of your shares will also increase. Another way to invest in the stock market is through ETFs (exchange-traded funds). ETFs bundle many shares of different companies in one fund and thus spread the risk. They are especially attractive to beginners because they are less volatile and offer wider diversification.

Tip: Start with small amounts and diversify your investments to minimize risk. Use platforms that have low fees and are user-friendly. Read financial news regularly and educate yourself constantly.

To enter the stock market, it is advisable to familiarize yourself with the basics of company analysis. Key figures such as the price-earnings ratio (P/E), the debt-to-equity ratio and historical price performance can provide information about a company's health and growth prospects. ETFs offer a good opportunity to invest broadly in the market without having to select individual stocks.

Real estate investments

Real estate is another excellent way to build wealth. The purchase of real estate can be used for personal use as well as for renting. Real estate offers the advantage of relatively stable performance and the opportunity to generate passive income through rental income.

Before investing in real estate, thorough market research is essential. The location of a property plays a decisive role in its performance. Urban development plans, infrastructure projects and the local economic situation can have a strong impact on long-term value development. In addition to the pure purchase price, you should also factor in ancillary costs such as real estate transfer tax, notary fees and brokerage fees. In the long term, rented properties offer a stable source of income, provided they are properly managed and maintained.

Tip: Before buying a property, think carefully about whether you want to use it yourself or rent it out. Calculate the potential rental income realistically and also take into account possible vacancy periods and maintenance costs.

Investments in your own business

One of the best investments you can make is in your own business. This can be in the form of equipment, marketing, training or personnel. By investing wisely in your business, you can not only increase your income, but also improve the efficiency and quality of your services or products.

Before making major investments in your business, it's important to create a detailed business plan. This should include not only the financial aspects, but also your long-term goals and market opportunities. Solid planning will help you maximize the return on your investments and minimize risks.

Tip: Regularly review the profitability of your investments and adjust your strategy as needed, and invest specifically in areas that offer the greatest potential for growth and profitability.

Balancing risk and return

No matter what type of investment you invest in, it's important to understand the risk/reward ratio. Higher returns often come with higher risks. Therefore, it is crucial to pursue a balanced strategy and not put all your eggs in one basket.

Tip: Use the principle of diversification to spread your risk. Don't invest in just one form of investment, but spread your capital across different investments. This allows you to minimize the risk of a total loss and increase your chances of long-term returns.

Education and continuous learning

Continuous training in finance and investment is essential. Books, online courses, seminars, and workshops can help you deepen your knowledge and stay up to date. One of my recommendations is the book "Rich Dad, Poor Dad" by Robert T. Kiyosaki, which has helped me personally a lot to better understand financial relationships.

Tip: Set fixed times for your further education and stick to a learning plan. Use podcasts and YouTube channels from financial experts to get inspired and get new ideas.

Final Thoughts

Investing is a marathon, not a sprint. It requires patience, discipline and constant learning. However, the rewards you can reap are enormous. Financial freedom and long-term prosperity are achievable not only through hard work, but also through smart and well-thought-out investments. Start investing today and take the first step towards a financially secure future.

With these insights and practical tips, I want to encourage you to actively pursue your financial goals and take control of your financial future. Invest in yourself, in your knowledge and in your future – it's the best decision you can make.

Chapter 8: Balancing Work and Leisure

Despite all professional ambitions, it is important to maintain the balance between work and leisure time. Success means not only financial freedom, but also the ability to live life to the fullest. In this chapter, I would like to show you how I find the balance between professional goals and personal recovery, and how you can achieve this too.

The importance of time-outs

The importance of time-outs cannot be overstated. To be successful in the long run, you need to learn when it's time to take a break. Breaks help to refresh the mind and recharge your batteries. They promote creativity and the ability to face challenges with a clear head.

Tip: Plan regular breaks and vacations. Use this time to switch off and concentrate on other things that bring you joy. Exercise, meditation or just spending time in nature can work wonders to clear your head and gain new perspectives.

Travel as a source of inspiration

I love to have beautiful holidays and discover new places. Traveling enriches my life and gives me new inspiration. No matter where I was, my laptop was always with me, and the will to move my business forward was always present. With this mindset, you can only win in the long run.

Tip: Use travel not only for relaxation, but also for inspiration. Visit business fairs, network meetings or workshops in other cities and countries to gain new perspectives and make valuable contacts. Often, the best ideas are born in a new environment or by exchanging ideas with people from different industries.

The role of family and partnership

The time with my girlfriend is very important to me, as she supports me a lot in all phases of my business. A strong partnership or supportive family environment is crucial for personal and professional success.

Tip: Consciously spend time with your loved ones. Be grateful for their support and share your successes and challenges with them. Strong emotional support can make all the difference in difficult times. At the same time, it is important to respect the needs of your family and your partnership and to find a healthy balance here as well.

Mindset and continuous growth

With the right mindset, you can only win in the long run. It is important to constantly work on yourself and develop yourself, both professionally and personally. This growth not only leads to more success in business, but also to a more fulfilling life.

Tip: Set both professional and personal goals. Work on your mindset by reading books, listening to podcasts, and attending seminars. Recognize that growth is an ongoing process. Self-reflection and the willingness to learn from mistakes are crucial for personal development and long-term success.

Integration of work and leisure time

One of the biggest challenges for entrepreneurs is to integrate work and leisure. The key is to use flexible working hours and locations to stay productive while also enjoying life.

Tip: Create a flexible work schedule that allows you to combine work and leisure. Use tools and apps to efficiently manage your work on the go. Prioritize tasks and set clear boundaries between work time and personal time to reduce stress and increase your productivity.

Final Thoughts

The balance between work and leisure time is crucial for sustainable success. It allows you to reach your full potential without burning out. Find what works best for you and be ready to adjust your strategies to find the perfect balance.

Success doesn't just mean achieving your professional goals, but also the ability to live life to the fullest. By taking time for relaxation and inspiration, you can increase your creativity and productivity and be successful in the long run. The art lies in finding the right balance that allows you to grow both professionally and personally and live a fulfilling life.

Chapter 9: Health and well-being

The more I did and the higher my professional ambitions grew, the more I realized how important health and well-being are. They became more and more important to me, because without them you can't really enjoy success. In this chapter, I want to show you how I take care of my health and why it is above all.

The importance of health

Health is the foundation for a successful life. Without it, all achievements and material successes are meaningless. Good health allows you to have the energy and focus to achieve your goals and reach your full potential.

Tip: Pay attention to regular health checks and listen to your body. Early detection and prevention are the key to a long and healthy life. Regular visits to the doctor, dentist appointments and check-ups help to identify and treat potential problems at an early stage.

Balanced diet

A balanced diet is essential for physical and mental well-being. I make sure to consume fresh and nutritious food. A diet rich in vitamins, minerals and antioxidants strengthens the immune system and keeps the body fit.

Tip: Plan your meals in advance and incorporate plenty of fruits, vegetables, whole grains and lean protein into your diet. Avoid processed foods and sugary drinks, which can lead to energy slumps and long-term health problems. Experiment with new recipes and foods to add variety to your diet.

Regular exercise

Regular exercise is another important building block for health. Sport not only helps to stay physically fit, but also to reduce stress and clear the mind. Whether it's an intense workout in the gym, a jog in the park or a relaxing yoga session – exercise should be an integral part of your everyday life.

Tip: Find a sport that you enjoy and integrate it into your daily routine. Set achievable goals and stay motivated by tracking your progress. Combine exercise with social activities, such as exercising with friends or family, for extra motivation and support.

Sufficient sleep

Sleep is often the underestimated factor for well-being and performance. Sufficient and high-quality sleep regenerates the body and strengthens the immune system. It is essential for mental clarity and productivity.

Tip: Establish a fixed sleep routine and ensure a relaxing sleeping environment. Avoid electronic devices before bedtime and use relaxing rituals such as reading or meditation to prepare your brain for sleep. Make sure to get enough hours of sleep per night, as lack of sleep can lead to health problems in the long term.

Mental balance and stress management

A healthy mind is just as important as a healthy body. Mental balance and effective stress management are crucial to mastering life's challenges. Techniques such as meditation, mindfulness, and breathing exercises can help calm the mind and reduce stress.

Tip: Take time for yourself every day to calm down and reflect. Find stress management methods that suit you and integrate them into your everyday life. Keeping a journal or meditating regularly can help center your mind and build emotional resilience.

Final Thoughts

Health and well-being are paramount. They are the foundation on which we build our lives and our success. By taking care of your health, you ensure that you have the energy and focus to achieve your goals and live your life to the fullest.

Success is only valuable if you can experience and enjoy it. Take care of your body and mind, and you'll find that you're more fulfilled and happier not only professionally, but also personally. Invest in your health by making conscious choices that lead to a healthy lifestyle in the long term.

Chapter 10: The Value of the Family

No matter how much money you have, health and family always come first for me. I really appreciate the time I spend with my family, and it gives me the strength to keep going. I dedicate this chapter to the most important people in my life and their inestimable value.

The source of love and support

Family is the source of love and support, backing up in difficult times and sharing joy in good times. They are the people who are always there for you, no matter what. This unconditional love and support is priceless and gives me the energy I need to pursue my dreams and achieve my goals.

Tip: Consciously take time for your family. Plan regular activities together, whether it's a dinner together, a weekend getaway, or just a cozy evening at home. These shared moments are valuable and strengthen family bonds. Make sure that this time is qualitative, for example by consciously putting your mobile phone and work aside in order to be fully present.

Success and family

Success is meaningless if you can't share it with the people who mean the most to you. It is important to find the right balance and ensure that the family is not neglected. The support of my family helped me overcome obstacles and keep going, even when it was difficult.

Tip: Integrate your family into your professional goals. Share your successes and challenges with them and share your journey with them. This creates a stronger understanding and a deeper connection. Show interest in your family members' activities and goals, and encourage them to pursue their dreams as well.

Gratitude and appreciation

The time I spend with my family is priceless. It is an opportunity to show gratitude and appreciation for their support and love. Without the unconditional love and support of my family, I would not be the person I am today.

Tip: Show your gratitude regularly. Small gestures of appreciation can go a long way. A handwritten letter, an unexpected gift, or just a heartfelt thank you can strengthen the bond with your loved ones. Make sure that your appreciation is genuine and sincere so that your family can show it
is really perceived.

Family time as a source of strength

The time spent together with my family gives me the strength to continue. These moments offer a welcome break from the hectic everyday life and allow me to relax and recharge my batteries. Whether it's a leisurely Sunday in the garden or a holiday together - these times are valuable and relaxing.

Tip: Create conscious time-outs for your family. Set clear boundaries between work and family time to ensure you're fully present when you're with your family. Avoid answering work calls or emails during this time to ensure undivided attention and quality in the shared moments.

Final Thoughts

Family is the foundation on which I build my life. It gives me the love, support, and motivation I need to succeed. That's why it's my top priority to cultivate relationships and enjoy the moments we share. Because at the end of the day, it's the people who mean the most to us who make our success truly valuable.

Success is more than financial success and professional achievements. It is the ability to live a fulfilled life, surrounded by the people who love and support us. By valuing and prioritizing our family, we ensure that our success matters and that our lives remain rich in love and joy.

Chapter 11: Tips and Tricks for Aspiring Entrepreneurs

In this chapter, I share practical advice for anyone who has the courage to pursue their own dreams. From idea to implementation – nothing is impossible if you believe in yourself and are willing to work hard.

The power of vision

Success is not a coincidence, but the result of hard work and smart decisions. It is important to always be clear why you started in the first place, even in difficult times, when everything and everyone seems against you and doubts arise. Write down your vision and motivation from the beginning in order to keep this drive in mind at all times.

Tip: Create a vision board. Collect images, quotes, and icons that represent your goals and dreams, and place it in a place where you see it every day. This will remind you of what you're working for and help you stay focused.

Motivation and goal setting

Every entrepreneur has his or her own motivation. Whether it's the desire for financial freedom, the urge to have a positive social impact, or a passion for a particular industry. It is important that you clearly define your motivation and make it visible in order to be able to motivate yourself again and again in difficult times.

Tip: Set clear, measurable goals. Use the SMART principle (Specific, Measurable, Achievable, Relevant, Time-bound) to formulate your goals and review them regularly. Stick to realistic time horizons and adjust your goals to new developments as needed.

Networking and building relationships

A strong network is an indispensable part of success. Relationships with other entrepreneurs, potential customers, and mentors can not only open up new business opportunities, but also provide valuable support and advice.

Tip: Participate regularly in networking events, be active in online forums and groups, and look specifically for mentors who can help you with their experience. Actively cultivate these relationships by not only asking for help, but also sharing support and knowledge yourself.

Continuous training

The business world is constantly changing. In order to be successful, it is important to always keep your finger on the pulse and to continuously educate yourself.

Tip: Invest in your education. Take part in workshops, seminars and online courses, read specialist books and journals. Podcasts and webinars also offer valuable opportunities to expand your knowledge and gain new perspectives.

Dealing with setbacks

Setbacks are part of being an entrepreneur, and they often offer the best learning opportunities. Dealing with mistakes and failures is crucial for long-term success.

Tip: See setbacks as an opportunity to learn and grow. Analyze what went wrong and develop strategies to be better prepared in the future. Stay flexible and adapt your strategies to new circumstances to become more resilient to challenges.

Financial management

Good financial management is the backbone of a successful business. Without a solid financial strategy, a business can quickly stumble.

Tip: Keep detailed accounting and prepare regular financial reports to keep track of income and expenses. Plan your expenses carefully and have an emergency fund ready to cover unforeseen costs and avoid liquidity bottlenecks.

Time management

Effective time management is crucial to managing the multitude of tasks that come with running your own business.

Tip: Use techniques like the Pomodoro Method to structure your work time and stay productive. Create daily to-do lists and prioritize your tasks according to urgency and importance. If possible, delegate tasks to employees or external service providers in order to use your own resources efficiently.

Customer Focus

The success of your business depends largely on how well you understand and meet the needs of your customers.

Tip: Collect feedback from your customers regularly, whether it's through surveys, face-to-face conversations, or reviews. Use this feedback constructively to continuously improve your products or services and adapt them to customer needs. Provide excellent customer service to build long-term relationships with your customers and earn their loyalty.

Personal resilience

The road to success is often rocky and requires mental strength and perseverance.

Tip: Take care of your mental health. Regularly practice stress management techniques such as meditation, breathing exercises, or sports to promote balance and resilience. Plan regular downtime to recover and recharge your batteries so that you stay focused even in challenging times.

Final thoughts

Being an entrepreneur requires courage, determination, and a clear vision. The journey may be challenging, but it also offers the opportunity to achieve your dreams and leave a lasting impact. With the right strategies and an unwavering belief in yourself, you too can achieve your goals and succeed.

Tip: Start now. Don't wait for the perfect moment, because there is no such thing. Put your ideas into action, learn from your experiences and always stay focused on your vision. The path may be rocky, but every step brings you closer to your goal.

<u>***Chapter 12: The Journey Continues***</u>

My path as an entrepreneur is far from over. The constant development and the pursuit of new goals keep me motivated and inspired. In this chapter, I take a look at my future plans and projects and invite you to join me on this exciting journey.

Diversification of income sources

Entrepreneurship is an endless learning process. New challenges and opportunities ensure that it never gets boring. For me, this means continuously expanding my business and opening up additional sources of income. In addition to my established online business, I have successfully built up another business area and am working on developing it further.

Tip: Identify your strengths and passions and use them to be successful. When you do something with enthusiasm, it also radiates to your customers and contributes to the long-term success of your company.

Integration of previous experiences

My experience as an insurance salesman has given me valuable knowledge in the field of customer service and sales. I have now successfully integrated these skills into my entrepreneurial portfolio. As an independent entrepreneur, I work for a significant client base and focus on their individual needs and the sustainable growth of my clientele.

Tip: Use previous work experience and skills to open up new business areas. Often, different skills can be profitably combined in a new context and expand your professional opportunities considerably.

Inspiring food for thought

I hope that my experiences and insights can provide inspiring food for thought for you. Every start into self-employment is unique and personal. It is crucial to continuously educate yourself and look for support. A mentor can provide valuable insight and support, while books and online resources provide the necessary knowledge.

Tip: Use social media and platforms like Instagram to connect with like-minded people and learn from their experiences. The exchange with other entrepreneurs can not only motivate, but also open up new perspectives and create valuable contacts.

Final Thoughts

The world of entrepreneurship is dynamic and offers endless opportunities for personal and professional growth. With a clear goal in mind and a willingness to learn from every experience, you too can make your journey successful. I look forward to continuing to document and share my journey with you. Feel free to follow me on my social channels, where I regularly give insights into my life and my business. Let's continue to grow together and make our dreams come true!

Tip: Start putting your vision into action today. Trust in your abilities and be willing to put in the necessary work. Each step brings you closer to your goal, so don't hesitate to get started and live your dream. Stay flexible and open to new opportunities, because often the greatest successes are where you least expect them.

Chapter 13: Scaling and Growing in E-Commerce

Scaling is crucial to succeed in e-commerce. In this chapter, we'll explore strategies for scaling your business on platforms like Amazon. We'll discuss how you can manage inventory to keep up with increasing demand, as well as the importance of logistics and fulfillment services. We'll also look at how you can achieve growth through targeted marketing and product innovation to expand your market presence.

Inventory management and demand forecasting

Efficient inventory management is a cornerstone of scaling in e-commerce. As your business grows, so does the complexity of inventory management. It's important to implement the right inventory strategies in a timely manner to avoid shortages while reducing excess inventory. Accurate demand forecasting based on historical sales data and seasonal trends can help keep the right amount of products in stock.

Technological solutions:

Use inventory management software that enables automated inventory updates and forecasts. These tools often offer features such as automatic reordering when stock levels are low and overstock alerts.

Just-in-Time (JIT) Supply Chain:

Implement JIT practices to optimize inventory levels and reduce capital commitment. By working closely with suppliers, you can ensure that you only receive goods when they are needed, thus reducing storage costs.

Dropshipping:

Consider the possibility of dropshipping for specific products. This can help you minimize inventory by shipping goods directly from the manufacturer or supplier to the customer, without the need for physical storage.

Logistics and Fulfillment

Effective logistics is crucial to deliver to customers on time and meet their expectations. Especially on platforms like Amazon, where fast delivery times and reliable fulfillment are important competitive advantages, a well-planned logistics strategy is essential.

Amazon Fulfillment by Amazon (FBA):

Use Amazon's FBA services to store, pack, and ship your products in Amazon warehouses. This not only enables fast delivery times, but also access to Amazon Prime customers and global markets.

Third-party fulfillment:

As an alternative to FBA, you can also work with external fulfillment service providers. These often offer tailor-made solutions that can better fit your specific requirements and cost structures.

Supply chain optimization:

Make sure your supply chain is efficient and that potential bottlenecks or delays are identified early. Proactively engage with suppliers and transport service providers to ensure a smooth movement of goods.

Targeted marketing for growth

Proper marketing plays a central role in scaling your ecommerce business. It's all about reaching your target audience, increasing your brand awareness, and increasing sales. Especially on Amazon, smart marketing is crucial to stand out from the competition and increase the visibility of your products.

Amazon PPC (Pay-Per-Click) Advertising:

Target paid advertising within Amazon. PPC campaigns can help you promote your products in search results and product pages to drive more clicks and conversions.

SEO Optimization for Amazon:

Improve the visibility of your product listings through a targeted SEO strategy. This includes using relevant keywords in titles, bullet points, and product descriptions, as well as optimizing images and videos to increase conversion rates.

Content Marketing and Social Media:

Use content marketing to build your brand and reach an engaged audience. Post useful content on your website, blogs, or social media that engages potential customers and inspires them to buy.

Product innovation and diversification

Continuously innovating and diversifying your product offering is critical to staying competitive in the long term and unlocking new market opportunities.

Market research and customer feedback:

Conduct regular market research to identify trends and understand customer needs. Use customer feedback to improve existing products or develop new products to meet demand.

Product variations and bundles:

Offer different product variations to cater to different customer preferences. Also, consider creating product bundles that can add value to customers while increasing the average order value.

Scaling through private labeling:

Consider the possibility of private labeling by developing your own branded products. This allows you to achieve unique positioning in the market and improve margins while maintaining control over product quality and brand image.

Case studies and best practices

To illustrate the theoretical concepts in a practical way, let's look at successful case studies of e-commerce companies that have successfully scaled. We analyze their strategies, challenges, and success factors to learn valuable lessons for your own business.

Summary and outlook

Scaling in e-commerce requires a strategic approach and continuous adaptation to changing market conditions. By effectively using inventory management, logistics, marketing strategies, and product innovation, you can successfully grow your business on platforms like Amazon. Stay flexible, learn from the experiences of other successful companies and adapt your strategies accordingly to ensure long-term success.

Chapter 14: Internationalization and Global E-Commerce

Selling on international markets offers enormous opportunities, but it also poses challenges. In this chapter, we'll explore how to successfully position your products on global e-commerce platforms like Amazon. We shed light on the legal and logistical aspects of international shipping as well as the cultural differences in marketing and customer approach. We also look at strategies for currency and pricing as well as adapting your products to different markets around the world.

Advantages of internationalization

Internationalizing your e-commerce business offers numerous benefits. It opens up new markets, diversifies your revenue potential, and mitigates the risk associated with reliance on a single market. With access to a global customer base, you can accelerate your company's growth and stabilize it in the long term.

Expansion of the customer base: By selling on international markets, you reach a wider target group. This can lead to a significant increase in your sales and a stronger brand presence.

Diversification of revenue streams: Selling in different geographic regions helps to spread market risks. A decline in demand in one market can be offset by strong growth in another.

Competitive advantage: Internationalization can give your company a competitive advantage by opening up new markets and positioning your brand globally.

Market research and market analysis

Before expanding into international markets, thorough market research and analysis is essential. This includes studying the demand for your products, analyzing the competition, and understanding market conditions in the target regions.

Needs assessment: Analyze the demand for your products in the target markets. Use tools like Google Trends, Amazon Best Seller Ranks, and local market research reports to evaluate the popularity and potential of your products.

Competitor analysis: Examine the competitors in the target markets. Identify their strengths and weaknesses and find out how you can differentiate yourself to gain a competitive advantage.

Market conditions: Understand the economic, political and legal framework in the target markets. Consider factors such as taxes, duties, import regulations, and the general economic situation to make informed decisions.

Legal and logistical aspects

Internationalizing your e-commerce business requires a comprehensive understanding of the legal and logistical challenges associated with international shipping and selling.

Legal requirements: Find out about the legal requirements in the target markets. This includes duties and taxes, import and export regulations, and consumer protection laws. Work closely with international trade advisors and lawyers to ensure you're compliant.

Logistics and shipping: Develop an efficient logistics strategy for international shipping. Use the services of global logistics providers like DHL, FedEx, and UPS to ensure smooth delivery. Also, consider the possibility of using fulfillment services like Amazon FBA to streamline your shipping processes.

Warehousing: Consider whether it makes sense to maintain warehouses in the target markets to shorten delivery times and reduce shipping costs. While setting up local warehouses can come at an additional cost, it offers significant benefits in terms of customer satisfaction and competitiveness.

Cultural Adaptation and Marketing Strategies

Success in international markets depends largely on how well you understand the cultural differences and adapt your marketing strategies accordingly.

Cultural differences: Each region has its own cultural norms and preferences. Tailor your marketing messages, product packaging, and advertising strategies to the cultural realities of the target markets, and use local experts and agencies to ensure your messages are effective and culturally sensitive.

Language and localization: Make sure your website and product descriptions are available in local languages. Use professional translation services to ensure high-quality, accurate localization. Not only does this improve the user experience, but it also increases the likelihood that potential customers will gain trust in your brand.

Social media and advertising: Use local social media platforms and ad networks to reach your target audience. In some markets, platforms such as WeChat, VKontakte or TikTok are more popular than Facebook or Instagram. Tailor your ad campaigns to target markets' preferred channels and formats.

Currency and pricing

Currency and pricing is another important aspect of internationalization. Strategic pricing helps you stay competitive while maximizing your profit margins.

Currency management: Accept payments in the local currencies of the target markets. Use payment processors like PayPal, Stripe, or Adyen to support multiple currencies and minimize exchange rate fluctuations.

Pricing strategy: Develop a flexible pricing strategy that takes into account purchasing power and competitive conditions in target markets. Consider setting different prices for different regions to meet local market demands. Also, take advantage of discounts and promotions to make it easier to enter the market and make your products more attractive.

Transparency: Make sure that all prices and fees are communicated transparently and clearly. Avoid hidden costs that could turn off potential customers and provide clear information about shipping costs, taxes, and duties.

Adapting products to different markets

Adapting your products to the needs and preferences of the target markets is crucial to success. This includes functional adjustments as well as changes in packaging and presentation.

Product specifications: Adapt your products to local standards and regulations. This may include technical adaptations, certifications, or compliance with certain safety standards.

Packaging: Design product packaging to match the cultural and aesthetic preferences of the target markets. This can include adjustments in terms of colors, symbols, and information on the packaging.

Product offerings: Develop special product variants or bundles for different markets. Consider local taste preferences, seasonal trends, and cultural specifics to create tailored offerings.

Customer Service and After-Sales Support

Excellent customer service is a crucial factor for success in international markets. Make sure you offer reliable and multilingual customer service to meet the expectations of your international customers.

Multilingual support: Provide customer service in the local languages of the target markets, using professional translators and customer service representatives to ensure that queries and issues are dealt with effectively and in a timely manner.

After-sales support: Make sure you offer robust after-sales support that covers repairs, returns, and refunds. Consider local consumer protection laws and regulations.

Customer satisfaction: Collect feedback from your international customers on a regular basis and use it to continuously improve your products and services. High customer satisfaction is crucial to promote long-term customer loyalty and positive word-of-mouth.

Summary and outlook

Internationalization in e-commerce offers enormous growth opportunities, but it requires careful planning and implementation. By conducting market research, overcoming legal and logistical challenges, making cultural adjustments, and developing strategic pricing, you can successfully scale your business globally. Stay flexible, learn from the experiences of other successful companies and adapt your strategies accordingly to ensure long-term success in international markets.

Chapter 15: Amazon SEO and Product Placement

The visibility of your products on Amazon is crucial for success. In this chapter, we'll go into detail about Amazon SEO (Search Engine Optimization) and how to optimize your product listings to be found more easily in search results. We discuss relevant key factors such as keywords, product descriptions, image optimization, and customer reviews. We also look at strategies for placing your products in relevant categories and on the Amazon search results page.

The Importance of Amazon SEO

Amazon is one of the largest e-commerce marketplaces in the world, and its search engine is key to the visibility of your products. Unlike general search engines like Google, Amazon has a specific search algorithm that aims to present the most relevant and most buyable products. Therefore, it is imperative that your product listings are optimized for Amazon search.

Goal of Amazon SEO: The main goal of Amazon SEO is to improve the ranking of your products in search results to increase visibility and maximize sales opportunities. The higher your product appears in search results, the more likely potential customers are to see and buy it.

Key Factors for Amazon SEO

1. Keywords: Keywords are the foundation of any SEO strategy. They help Amazon categorize your products and match them to the right search queries. Thorough keyword research is therefore essential.

Keyword research: Use tools like Amazon's Autocomplete, Amazon's Search Term Tool, and external keyword tools like Helium 10, Jungle Scout, or MerchantWords to identify relevant keywords. Look for keywords that have high search volume and low competition.

Keyword placement: Include the most important keywords in the product title, bullet points, product description, and backend keywords. However, avoid keyword stuffing, as it can lead to a poor user experience and potential penalties from Amazon.

2. Product Title: The product title is one of the most important SEO factors on Amazon. It should be concise, informative, and include the most important keywords.

Product title best practices: Keep the title under 200 characters and start with the most important information, such as brand name, product name, and key features. Avoid superfluous words and make sure the title is easy to read.

3. Bullet Points: The bullet points are the short descriptions that highlight important product information. They should be clear and concise, emphasizing the benefits of the product.

Bullet Point Optimization: Use bullet points to highlight the key features and benefits of your product. Include relevant keywords, but make sure the information is understandable and engaging.

4. Product Description: The product description provides the opportunity to provide detailed information about your product. It should be well-structured and easy to read.

Product description optimization: Use HTML formatting to create paragraphs, lists, and bold text. This improves readability and user experience. Integrate important keywords naturally and avoid excessive repetition.

5. Images: High-quality images are crucial for conversion rates. You should show the product from different angles and in high resolution.

Image optimization: Upload at least seven images, including a main image and six additional images that show different aspects of the product. Also, use lifestyle images that show the product in use to better engage potential buyers.

6. Customer reviews: Positive reviews and high star ratings are crucial for success on Amazon. They not only influence customers' purchasing decisions, but also their placement in search results.

Strategies to improve customer reviews: Encourage honest customer feedback by providing excellent customer service and exceeding customer expectations. Also, use Amazon's Early Reviewer Program and Vine program to get more reviews.

Product Placement Strategies

Categorization: Proper categorization of your products is crucial for visibility. Make sure your products are listed in the most relevant categories and subcategories.

Optimize categorization: Use Amazon's product catalog to find the most accurate and relevant categories for your products. Incorrect or inaccurate categorization can negatively affect the visibility and discoverability of your products.

Backend keywords: Backend keywords are keywords that are entered into Seller Central and are visible to the search engine but invisible to customers. They offer the possibility of integrating additional relevant keywords.

Backend keyword optimization: Fill in all available characters for backend keywords and use different keyword variations, including synonyms and alternate spellings. Avoid repetition and unnecessary punctuation.

A+ Content: A+ Content (also known as enhanced brand content) offers the ability to create advanced content such as detailed product descriptions, comparison charts, and high-quality images.

Benefits of A+ Content: A+ Content can increase conversions by providing more detailed and engaging information. This helps to better inform and persuade potential buyers.

Amazon Advertising: Use Amazon's advertising platform to increase the visibility of your products. Sponsored Products, Sponsored Brands, and Display Ads can help get your products in front of a larger audience.

Amazon Advertising Strategies: Use targeted advertising campaigns to increase visibility and sales. Use data analytics tools to monitor and optimize the performance of your ads.

Practical examples and best practices

To illustrate the theoretical concepts, let's look at successful case studies and best practices from companies that have effectively used Amazon SEO to increase their visibility and sales.

Case Study: XYZ Company's Successful Amazon SEO Strategies

Keyword Strategy: How did XYZ Company identify relevant keywords and integrate them into their product listings?

Product Listing Optimization: What techniques did the company use to optimize product titles, bullet points, and product descriptions?

Image optimization: What kind of images did XYZ Company use to improve their conversion rate?

Customer reviews: What strategies has the company used to receive and maintain positive reviews?

Summary and outlook

Amazon SEO and product placement are crucial for success in e-commerce. By optimizing keywords, product descriptions, images, and customer reviews, you can increase the visibility of your products and maximize sales opportunities. Stay up-to-date on the latest SEO trends and Amazon guidelines to continuously improve your strategies. With a well-thought-out and well-executed SEO strategy, you can take your Amazon business to the next level and ensure long-term success.

Chapter 16: Customer Reviews and Reputation on Different Platforms

Customer reviews play a central role in e-commerce, especially on platforms like Amazon. In this chapter, we'll explore how to gain positive customer reviews and build your reputation as a seller. We discuss best practices for interacting with customers, responding to feedback, and resolving problems. We'll also look at the legal aspects of reviews and how to effectively address negative reviews to build customer trust.

The importance of customer reviews

Customer reviews are the backbone of trust in e-commerce. They have a significant influence on the purchasing decisions of potential customers and are a decisive factor in the placement of your products in Amazon search results. Positive reviews can significantly increase sales, while negative reviews can do the opposite.

Goal of customer reviews: The main goal is to get authentic and positive feedback that reflects the quality of your products and services. Customer reviews not only help attract new customers, but also provide valuable insights into customer satisfaction and areas for improvement.

Strategies for Attracting Positive Customer Reviews

Outstanding customer service: Excellent customer service is key to customer satisfaction and positive reviews. Take care of your customers' needs and exceed their expectations.

Customer service best practices: Respond quickly to customer inquiries, be friendly and helpful, and resolve issues efficiently. A positive customer experience often leads to positive reviews.

Follow-up emails: After the purchase is the ideal time to ask customers for a review. Follow-up emails are an effective way to get feedback.

Optimize follow-up emails: Send personalized and friendly follow-up emails and politely ask for a review. Remind customers how important their feedback is to you.

Interaction with customers and feedback management

Active communication: Communication is key to maintaining good customer relationships. Respond quickly and professionally to customer inquiries and feedback.

Strategies for effective communication: Always be friendly, helpful and solution-oriented. Proactive communication can prevent many potential problems.

Solving problems: No product is perfect, and occasionally problems arise. How you deal with these issues can make all the difference.

Problem-solving best practices: Listen carefully to customers, acknowledge the problem, and provide quick and satisfying solutions. Show empathy and understanding to gain the trust of customers.

Reply to reviews: Respond to all reviews, both positive and negative. This shows that you value your customers' feedback and take it seriously.

Optimize responses: Thank customers for positive reviews and address specific points. In the case of negative reviews, show understanding, apologize and offer a solution.

Legal aspects of reviews

Amazon has strict guidelines to ensure the authenticity of customer reviews. It's important to understand and comply with these guidelines to avoid legal issues and protect your reputation.

Feedback manipulation: Any attempt to manipulate reviews is strictly prohibited and can result in serious consequences, including suspension of your seller account.

Avoid review manipulation: Don't buy reviews or offer incentives in exchange for positive reviews, and use legitimate programs like the Early Reviewer Program and Vine.

Honest feedback: Make sure all reviews are honest and authentic. Encourage your customers to share their real experiences.

Transparency and authenticity: Be transparent in your business practices and encourage honest feedback. Authentic reviews are more valuable and credible.

Dealing with negative reviews

Negative reviews are inevitable, but dealing with them can have a huge impact on your business. Here are some strategies to effectively handle negative reviews.

Stay calm and respond objectively: It's important to respond to negative reviews calmly and objectively. Avoid reacting emotionally.

Response best practices: Thank them for the feedback, apologize for the inconvenience, and offer a solution.

Solve problems internally: Use negative reviews as a learning opportunity to improve internal processes and product quality.

Internal evaluation: Analyze negative reviews to identify and address recurring issues. This will help prevent future discomfort.

Proactive management: Proactive review management can help minimize negative reviews.

Proactive measures: Contact unhappy customers directly before they leave a negative review and offer a solution. This can prevent a lot of negative reviews.

Building a strong reputation on

A strong reputation as a salesperson can help you gain customer trust and increase your sales.

Consistent quality: Consistently offer high-quality products and services to earn and maintain your customers' trust.

Quality control: Implement strict quality control processes to ensure that your products meet customer expectations.

Transparent business processes: Be transparent in your business processes, from product description to customer service.

Transparency and honesty: Communicate openly with your customers and make sure that all product information is accurate and comprehensive.

Brand building: Invest in building your brand to drive long-term customer loyalty.

Brand strategy: Develop a strong brand identity and message that fosters trust and loyalty with your customers.

Summary and outlook

Customer reviews and reputation are critical to success on Amazon. Through excellent customer service, effective communication, and proactive review management, you can gain positive reviews and build your reputation as a seller. Adhere to legal guidelines and encourage honest feedback to earn and maintain your customers' trust in the long term. With a well-thought-out strategy, you can unlock the full potential of your customer reviews and successfully grow your business on Amazon.

Chapter 17: Brand Building and Branding

A strong brand is a competitive advantage in e-commerce. In this chapter, you'll learn how to build a brand and optimize your branding on Amazon. We'll discuss strategies for creating a consistent brand image, creating engaging product pages, and leveraging Amazon Brand Registry. We'll also look at the importance of brand protection and how you can protect your brand from counterfeits and unauthorized sellers.

The importance of a strong brand

In the competitive environment of e-commerce, a strong brand can make all the difference. A brand is more than just a logo or a name – it represents the identity, values and quality of a company. By building a recognizable and trustworthy brand, businesses can gain customer loyalty and stand out from the competition.

Protecting your brand

Brand protection is an essential aspect of brand building. Counterfeits and unauthorized sales can not only hurt your sales, but also erode customer trust in your brand.

Summary and outlook

Building a strong brand on Amazon requires a thoughtful strategy and continuous efforts. By creating a consistent brand image, optimizing your product pages, and using Amazon Brand Registry, you can strengthen your brand and earn customer trust. Protecting your brand is just as important to ensure long-term success. With the right strategies, you can overcome the challenges of brand protection and build your brand sustainably.

Chapter 18: Paid Advertising and PPC Campaigns

Paid advertising on Amazon, Google, META and Co. can significantly increase your sales. In this chapter, we'll look at the basics of PPC (Pay-Per-Click) campaigns and how to create effective ads on Amazon. We'll discuss different types of ads, such as Sponsored Products, Sponsored Brands, and Sponsored Display Ads, as well as strategies for budgeting, keyword targeting, and campaign optimization. We'll also look at tools and analytics to maximize the ROI of your ad spend.

The basics of PPC (Pay-Per-Click) campaigns

Pay-Per-Click (PPC) campaigns are an essential part of the advertising strategy on Amazon. With PPC, you only pay when a potential customer clicks on your ad. This makes PPC a cost-effective way to increase the visibility of your products and generate targeted traffic.

Summary and outlook

Paid advertising and PPC campaigns are powerful tools to increase the visibility of your products and increase sales. Through careful planning, targeted keyword targeting, and continuous optimization, you can make your campaigns successful and maximize ROI. Use the tools and analytics at your disposal to make data-driven decisions and continuously improve your advertising strategies. With the right strategies and consistent implementation, you can take full advantage of PPC advertising on Amazon and strengthen your market position.

Chapter 19: Crisis Management and Challenges in E-Commerce

Crises can affect any company, even in e-commerce. In this chapter, we explore best practices and strategies for crisis management in e-commerce. We look at scenarios such as logistics issues, product recalls, negative PR, and legal challenges. We discuss how to proactively respond to crises, develop communication strategies with customers and stakeholders, and make your business resilient to unforeseen events.

Introduction to crisis management in e-commerce

E-commerce businesses are particularly vulnerable to crises due to their reliance on technology, logistics networks, and global markets. Effective crisis management is therefore essential to ensure stability and customer trust in your business.

Why crisis management is important:

Trust and reputation: Reacting quickly and transparently to crises helps to maintain customer trust and protect reputation.

Continuity: Effective crisis management ensures that your business continues to run even in difficult times and that lost sales are minimized.

Resilience: Preparation and planning increase your company's resilience to future crises.

Identification of potential crises in e-commerce

The first step in crisis management is to identify potential crises that could affect your e-commerce business. Here are some common scenarios:

Logistics problems:
Causes: delivery problems, delays at shipping service providers or failures in the supply chain.
Impact: Late deliveries, unhappy customers, and potential revenue losses.

Product recalls:
Causes: Product defects, safety concerns, or regulatory violations.
Impact: Cost of recall, negative PR, and loss of customer trust.

Negative PR:
Causes: Poor customer feedback, scandals, or defective products.
Impact: Reputational damage and potential decline in sales.

Legal challenges:
Causes: Regulatory violations, patent disputes, or data protection violations.
Impact: Legal costs, fines and negative media coverage.

Proactive measures for crisis prevention

Proactive measures can help prevent potential crises or minimize their impact. Here are some strategies to prepare:

1. Risk assessment:
Analysis: Conduct a comprehensive risk assessment to identify potential vulnerabilities and threats.
Prioritization: Categorize risks according to their probability and potential impact.

2. Contingency plans:
Development: Create contingency plans for various crisis scenarios, including detailed steps and responsibilities.
Exercises: Conduct regular crisis simulations and exercises to prepare your team for the worst-case scenario.

3. Communication strategies:
Protocols: Develop communication protocols for internal and external exchanges during a crisis.
Transparency: Rely on transparent and timely communication to maintain the trust of customers and stakeholders.

4. Monitoring and early warning systems:
Tools: Use monitoring tools to identify potential crises at an early stage (e.g. social media monitoring, logistics tracking).
Indicators: Define key indicators that could indicate potential problems.

Crisis response

When a crisis occurs, quick and deliberate action is crucial. Here are the steps to respond effectively to a crisis:

1. Activate the crisis team:
Composition: Assemble a crisis team consisting of members from all relevant departments (e.g. logistics, customer service, PR, legal).
Responsibilities: Clarify the responsibilities and communication channels within the team.

2. Evaluate the situation:
Collect data: Gather all available information about the crisis to get a clear picture of the situation.
Assessment: Analyze the data to understand the scale and potential impact of the crisis.

3. Take action:
Immediate measures: Implement immediate measures to contain the crisis (e.g. shipping stops, recalls).
Long-term solutions: Develop long-term solutions to address the root causes of the crisis and prevent future incidents.

4. Communication:
Internal: Inform all employees about the crisis and the measures taken.
External: Communicate transparently with customers, partners, and the public. Use all available channels to provide timely information.

Case studies and examples

To illustrate the theoretical concepts, let's look at some case studies of companies that have successfully responded to crises in e-commerce:

Case Study: XYZ E-Commerce Company

Crisis: XYZ Company had to deal with a massive logistics outage that led to significant delivery delays.
Reaction: The company immediately activated its crisis team, informed all affected customers transparently and offered compensation in the form of vouchers.
Result: By acting quickly and transparently, the company was able to maintain the trust of customers to a large extent and overcome the crisis.

Case Study: ABC Online Store

Crisis: ABC Online Store was confronted with a product recall due to safety defects.
Reaction: The store carried out the recall professionally, communicated openly about the reasons and ensured that affected customers received replacements quickly.
Result: Despite the recall, ABC Online Store was able to maintain customer loyalty and strengthen trust in the brand through proactive crisis management.

Long-term resilience and learning from crises

After overcoming a crisis, it is important to learn from the experience and take measures to strengthen long-term resilience:

1. Evaluation and analysis:

Review: Conduct a thorough follow-up analysis to understand what went well and where there is room for improvement.
Learn: Document the lessons learned from the crisis and incorporate them into future contingency plans and strategies.

2. Optimization of processes:

Improvements: Identify and implement process improvements to increase your organization's efficiency and responsiveness.
Innovation: Use the crisis as an opportunity to integrate innovative solutions and technologies that strengthen your resilience.

3. Training:
Training: Conduct regular training and workshops for your team to improve their crisis management skills.

Participation: Foster a culture of open communication and participation, where employees are encouraged to report potential risks early.

Summary and outlook

Crisis management is an indispensable part of e-commerce. By taking proactive measures, clear communication strategies, and continuously optimizing your processes, you can make your business more resilient and maintain your customers' trust. Use the strategies and tools described in this chapter to prepare for possible crises and respond effectively. This will ensure that your e-commerce business remains stable and successful even during turbulent times.

This chapter provides a comprehensive guide to crisis management in e-commerce. It includes practical advice, case studies, and strategies to help you identify potential crises, respond proactively to them, and make your business more resilient to unforeseen events.

Chapter 20: Trends and Innovations in E-Commerce

E-commerce is constantly evolving. In this chapter, we explore current trends and innovations that are shaping the future of e-commerce. We look at topics such as AI and machine learning in e-commerce, personalization of shopping experiences, voice commerce, and the integration of augmented reality (AR) and virtual reality (VR). We will also discuss how you as an entrepreneur can use these technologies to strengthen your competitive position and inspire customers.

Introduction to the trends and innovations in e-commerce

The dynamics of e-commerce require entrepreneurs to be constantly adaptable and innovative. With the rapid development of new technologies, new opportunities to improve the shopping experience and increase efficiency are constantly emerging. In this chapter, we look at the most significant trends and technologies that are revolutionizing online retail.

Artificial Intelligence (AI) and Machine Learning

AI and machine learning have the potential to fundamentally change e-commerce by creating personalized shopping experiences and optimizing business processes.

Applications of AI and machine learning:

1. Personalized recommendations:
Algorithms: AI-powered algorithms analyze customers' behavior and recommend products that match their preferences and previous purchases.

Result: This leads to higher customer satisfaction and increases sales through cross- and upselling.

2. Chatbots and customer service:
24/7 support: AI-powered chatbots provide round-the-clock support and answer frequently asked questions quickly and efficiently.
Improvement: This improves customer retention and reduces the burden on the customer service team.

3. Price optimization:
Dynamic pricing: AI algorithms analyze market trends and competitor prices to set optimal prices in real-time.
Advantage: This maximizes sales and increases competitiveness.

4. Inventory Management:
Forecasting: Machine learning can analyze sales data and make accurate predictions about future inventory requirements.
Efficiency: This reduces storage costs and prevents out-of-stock situations.

Personalization of shopping experiences

Personalization is a key trend in e-commerce that can significantly improve the customer experience. By leveraging data and technology, tailored shopping experiences can be created.

Personalization strategies:

1. Individual product suggestions:
Data analysis: By analyzing customer data, personalized product suggestions can be made that are tailored to the customer's individual tastes.
Result: This leads to a higher conversion rate and strengthens customer loyalty.

2. Personalized marketing campaigns:
Segmentation: Audience-specific campaigns can be created by segmenting the customer base based on demographic and behavioral data.
Success: This increases the relevance of marketing messages and improves campaign performance.

3. Individualized e-mails:
Customization: Email campaigns can be personalized by addressing the customer's past purchase history and preferences.
Benefit: This increases open and click-through rates, as well as customer loyalty.

Voice Commerce

Voice commerce, i.e. shopping by voice command, is becoming increasingly important. With the proliferation of smart speakers such as Amazon Echo and Google Home, this type of shopping is becoming increasingly popular.

Advantages of voice commerce:

1. Convenience:
Easy to use: Customers can order products quickly and conveniently by voice command without having to manually operate a device.
Result: This increases customer satisfaction and encourages spontaneous purchases.

2. Accessibility:
Accessibility: Voice commerce offers barrier-free shopping for people with physical disabilities.
Inclusion: This expands the potential customer base and increases market reach.

3. Technology Integration:
Linkage: Voice commerce can be seamlessly integrated with other technologies such as smart home devices and AI systems.
Synergy: This creates a connected and streamlined shopping experience.

Augmented Reality (AR) and Virtual Reality (VR)

AR and VR offer innovative ways to enrich the online shopping experience and provide customers with an immersive shopping experience.

Applications of AR and VR in e-commerce:

1. Virtual try-on:
AR tools: Customers can virtually try on clothes and accessories to see how they look on them before making a purchase decision.
Advantage: This reduces returns and increases customer satisfaction.

2. Product visualization:
3D models: Products can be presented as 3D models that customers can view from all angles and project into their own environment.
Result: This improves the understanding of the product and promotes the completion of the purchase.

3. Virtual showrooms:
VR experience: Businesses can create virtual showrooms where customers can discover and interact with products in an immersive environment.
Experience: This provides a unique and engaging shopping experience that stands out from traditional online stores.

Sustainability and environmentally conscious e-commerce

Sustainability is increasingly becoming an important topic in e-commerce. Customers are placing more and more emphasis on eco-friendly practices and sustainable products.

Strategies for sustainable e-commerce:

1. Sustainable products:
Product range: Offer products that have been produced in an environmentally friendly way and are made of sustainable materials.
Advantage: This appeals to environmentally conscious customers and strengthens brand reputation.

2. Eco-friendly packing:
Packaging materials: Use recyclable or biodegradable packaging materials.
Result: This reduces the ecological footprint of your company and meets with a positive response from customers.

3. Climate-neutral shipping:
Offsetting: Offer climate-neutral shipping by offsetting CO_2 emissions through climate protection projects.
Benefit: This positions your business as environmentally conscious and improves customer image.

Blockchain technology in e-commerce

Blockchain technology has numerous applications in e-commerce, from improving transparency to securing transactions.

Applications of blockchain in e-commerce:

1. Supply Chain Transparency:
Tracking: Blockchain can be used to transparently track the entire supply chain of a product.
Advantage: This strengthens customers' trust in the origin and authenticity of the products.

2. Secure payments:
Transactions: Blockchain-based payment systems offer secure and fast transactions without intermediaries.
Result: This reduces transaction costs and increases payment security.

3. Smart contracts:
Automation: Smart contracts allow contract terms to be automatically executed once certain criteria are met.
Efficiency: This increases efficiency and reduces administrative overhead.

Artificial intelligence in customer service

AI can also revolutionize customer service by providing fast and efficient support and increasing customer satisfaction.

Applications of AI in customer service:

1. Chatbots and virtual assistants:
24/7 support: AI-powered chatbots can answer questions and solve problems around the clock.
Efficiency: This takes the pressure off the customer service team and provides immediate help to customers.

2. Personalized Support:
Data analytics: AI can analyze customer data and provide personalized support based on customers' unique needs.
Result: This improves the customer experience and increases customer loyalty.

3. Automated emails:
Responses: AI can create automatic email responses that address frequently asked questions and include personalized recommendations.
Benefit: This speeds up response time and improves customer service efficiency.

Summary and outlook

E-commerce is an ever-changing field characterized by technological innovations and changing customer demands. The trends and technologies we've explored in this chapter offer numerous opportunities to improve the shopping experience and increase the efficiency of your business. By leveraging these innovations, you can strengthen your competitive position and delight your customers. Always stay open to new developments and be ready to adapt and innovate your business to stay successful in the dynamic world of e-commerce.

Chapter 21: Sustainability and ethical e-commerce

Sustainability and ethical practices are becoming increasingly important in e-commerce. In this chapter, we explore how you as an entrepreneur can integrate sustainable principles into your business model. We discuss environmentally friendly packaging, CO_2-neutral delivery options, fair working conditions in the supply chain and transparent communication with customers. We also look at certifications and standards for sustainable e-commerce as well as the growing importance of corporate social responsibility (CSR).

Introduction to sustainable and ethical e-commerce

Sustainability and ethical action are not only ethically imperative, but also economically sensible. In e-commerce, companies can strengthen their competitiveness through sustainable practices while making a positive contribution to the environment and society. This chapter examines various aspects and strategies of how companies can integrate sustainable principles to ensure long-term success.

Eco-friendly packaging in e-commerce

Eco-friendly packaging is an essential part of sustainable e-commerce. The choice of packaging materials and the reduction of waste play a crucial role in a company's environmental footprint.

Strategies for eco-friendly packaging:

1. Recyclable materials: Use packaging materials that are recyclable and have a low environmental footprint.
Example: cardboard, paper and biodegradable plastics.

2. Reduce packaging waste: Minimize the size of the packaging and avoid excessive packaging materials.
Advantage: This not only reduces costs, but also the ecological footprint.

3. Biodegradable packaging: Rely on packaging materials that are biodegradable and can be disposed of in an environmentally friendly way.
Sustainability: This supports a circular economy and reduces environmental impact.

4. Reusable packaging: Implement systems for customers to return and reuse packaging materials.
Customer benefit: This promotes customer loyalty and shows commitment to sustainable action.

CO_2-neutral delivery options and logistics

The transport and delivery of goods has a significant impact on the environment. Companies can reduce their environmental footprints by using CO_2-neutral delivery options and optimizing logistics chains.

Measures for CO_2-neutral delivery options:

1. Alternative delivery methods: Use alternative means of transport such as electric vehicles, bike couriers or eco-friendly delivery services.
Reduction of emissions: This minimizes greenhouse gas emissions and supports climate protection goals.

2. Offsetting CO_2 emissions: Offset CO_2 emissions by investing in climate protection projects or buying CO_2 certificates.
Sustainability: This enables an environmentally friendly supply chain and improves the company's image.

3. Efficient route planning: Optimize route planning for deliveries to minimize driving distances and reduce fuel consumption.
Cost savings: This reduces transportation costs and improves the efficiency of logistics operations.

Fair working conditions in the supply chain

Compliance with fair working conditions along the entire supply chain is a central aspect of ethical action in e-commerce. Companies have a responsibility to ensure that all actors involved in manufacturing and delivery receive decent working conditions and fair remuneration.

Measures for fair working conditions:

1. Supplier review and audit: Regularly check suppliers for compliance with internationally recognized labor standards and conduct audits.

Transparency: This ensures compliance with ethical standards and minimizes the risk of labor rights violations.

2. Training and education: Educate suppliers and employees in the supply chain on labor rights and standards.

Partnership: This promotes long-term partnerships and strengthens cooperation along the supply chain.

3. Engage in sustainable practices: Integrate compliance with fair working conditions into sourcing policies and contracts with suppliers.

Responsibility: This shows commitment to social responsibility and strengthens the company's image.

Transparent communication with customers

Transparency is crucial to gaining customer trust and building long-term relationships. Through transparent communication, companies can make their sustainability efforts clear and promote customer awareness of ethical consumption.

Best practices for transparent communication:

1. Sustainability reporting: Publish regular reports on the company's sustainability performance and progress on green initiatives.

Customer loyalty: This builds customer trust and demonstrates commitment to sustainable action.

2. Clear product labeling: Label products with eco-friendly features and certifications to make it easier for ethical consumers to choose.

Transparency: This supports informed purchasing decisions and shows a commitment to sustainability.

3. Customer communication: Inform customers about sustainable practices, such as CO2-neutral delivery options or eco-friendly packaging materials, during the ordering process.

Education: This raises customers' awareness of sustainability and increases their appreciation for ethical e-commerce.

Certifications and standards for sustainable e-commerce

Certifications and standards play an important role in increasing the credibility and transparency of companies in the field of sustainable e-commerce. They help companies validate their sustainability efforts and gain consumer trust.

Relevant certifications and standards:

1. Fair Trade: Certifications such as Fair Trade promote fair working conditions and fair remuneration for producers in developing countries.

Fairness: This supports fair trade and improves the living conditions of producer communities.

2. Ecological certifications: Labels such as the EU Ecolabel or the Blue Angel mark identify products that meet strict environmental standards.

Environmental protection: This shows the commitment to environmental protection and reduces the environmental footprint of the products.

3. Socially responsible procurement: Standards such as SA8000 establish guidelines for socially responsible procurement and labor practices.

Responsibility: This supports compliance with ethical standards along the entire supply chain and strengthens the company's image.

Corporate Social Responsibility (CSR) in E-Commerce

Corporate Social Responsibility (CSR) refers to the responsibility of companies towards society and the environment. In e-commerce, CSR can be a significant

by helping companies achieve positive social and environmental impact.

CSR measures in e-commerce:

1. Nonprofit partnerships: Engage in partnerships with nonprofits and help solve societal challenges.

Social commitment: This strengthens the company's image and promotes a sense of community.

2. Sustainable business practices: Implement sustainable business models and environmentally friendly initiatives that go beyond legal requirements.

Environmental awareness: This shows the commitment to environmental protection and sustainable development.

3. Ethics and governance: Integrate ethical principles into corporate governance and actively participate in the development of industry standards for ethical e-commerce.

Integrity: This fosters trust and credibility with customers and stakeholders.

Inference

Sustainability and ethical e-commerce are not just trends, but fundamental principles that will significantly shape the future of e-commerce. Companies that proactively advocate sustainable practices and uphold ethical standards are not only better positioned to meet rising consumer expectations, but can also benefit from increased brand loyalty and an improved corporate image in the long term. By driving the conversation around sustainable and ethical e-commerce and promoting best practices, together we can make a positive change for society and the environment.

This extended chapter provides a comprehensive overview of the importance and implementation of sustainability and ethical action in e-commerce.

To expand the chapter "Future Outlook: The Evolution of E-Commerce" to over 4000 words, I will delve deeper into the following topics and include additional relevant information.

Chapter 22: Future Outlook: The Evolution of E-Commerce

The future of e-commerce promises exciting developments. In this chapter, we take a look at future trends and challenges in online retail. We explore technologies such as blockchain for supply chain management, the impact of 5G on mobile shopping, and the growing role of big data and predictive analytics in e-commerce. In addition, we look at social and political factors that could shape online retail in the coming years.

Blockchain in supply chain management

Blockchain technology has the potential to radically transform e-commerce supply chains. Due to its decentralized and transparent nature, blockchain offers a solution to problems such as supply chain management, product traceability, and security.

Applications of blockchain in e-commerce:

1. Transparency and traceability: Blockchain enables end-to-end traceability of products along the entire supply chain, which creates trust among consumers.
Example: Companies can trace the origin of products all the way to the end consumer.

2. Security and privacy: The decentralized nature of blockchain reduces the risk of data manipulation and cyberattacks.
Benefit: This improves the security of sensitive information such as payment details and personal identities.

3. Smart contracts: Automated contracts enable efficient payment processing and contract management without intermediaries.
Efficiency: This reduces costs and speeds up transactions in the supply chain.

4. Building Trust: Blockchain-based systems promote trust between businesses, suppliers, and consumers through transparent business practices.
Sustainability: This supports sustainable practices and improves compliance along the supply chain.

Impact of 5G on mobile shopping

The introduction of 5G technology promises to revolutionize mobile shopping. Improved speed, lower latency and higher capacities open up new possibilities for personalized shopping experiences and immersive technologies.

Potentials of 5G in e-commerce:

1. Faster loading times: 5G enables faster website loading times and improves the user experience when shopping on mobile.
Customer satisfaction: This reduces abandonment rates and boosts conversion rates for mobile purchases.

2. Augmented Reality (AR) and Virtual Reality (VR): Higher bandwidths and lower latency support the integration of AR and VR into mobile shopping applications.
Immersive experiences: This allows customers to experience products virtually and drives purchasing decisions.

3. IoT and connected devices: 5G supports the connection and interaction of connected devices in e-commerce, such as smart home appliances and wearables.
Personalization: This opens up opportunities for personalized offers and automated ordering processes.

Big Data and Predictive Analytics in E-Commerce

Big data and predictive analytics are playing an increasingly important role in e-commerce, helping businesses make data-driven decisions, understand customer behavior, and deliver personalized shopping experiences.

Benefits of big data in e-commerce:

1. Customer Behavior Analysis: Big data allows for deeper analysis of customer behavior across different channels.
Segmentation: This allows customers to be segmented for targeted marketing actions and personalized recommendations.

2. Inventory management: Predictive models based on big data help optimize inventory levels and reduce excess inventory.
Efficiency: This reduces costs and improves warehousing.

3. Pricing and offer optimization: Predictive analytics predicts price changes and helps optimize promotions and discounts.
Competitiveness: This improves the competitive position and increases profitability.

4. Real-time analytics: Big data enables real-time analytics to respond quickly to market developments and customer feedback.

Agility: This supports agile business models and flexible adaptations to market changes.

Social and political influencing factors

E-commerce is increasingly influenced by social and political developments that can create regulatory challenges and new market conditions. Companies must adapt to these influencing factors and take strategic measures to adapt and seize opportunities.

Influencing factors in e-commerce:

1. Privacy and security: Legal frameworks and consumer protection laws influence data security and the handling of personal information.
2. Compliance:** This requires adherence to privacy policies and security standards.

2. Trade policy and international markets: Changes in trade policy and trade agreements can affect cross-border e-commerce.
Globalisation: This opens up new markets and requires adaptation to different legal frameworks.

3. Customer trust and ethics: Consumers increasingly value ethical business practices and transparency, which obliges companies to act responsibly.
Reputation: This affects brand image and customer loyalty.

4. Technological development and regulation: Governments are responding to technological developments in e-commerce with new laws and regulations.
Innovation: This promotes innovation and can reduce or increase market barriers.

Inference

A look into the future of e-commerce reveals a dynamic environment characterized by technological innovations, societal changes, and regulatory challenges. Companies that understand these developments and react proactively to them have the opportunity to strengthen their competitiveness and ensure long-term success. By focusing on the potentials of blockchain, 5G, big data and societal influencers, we can help shape the future of e-commerce and unlock new opportunities for growth and innovation.

Chapter 23: Summary and Conclusion

Congratulations! You've completed an exciting journey through the world of e-commerce, from the basics of starting a business to advanced strategies for scaling and expanding internationally. In this last chapter, we would like to summarize the most important findings.

Key takeaways from this guide

1. Starting and building an e-commerce business**: You've learned the importance of building a strong brand and strategically positioning your products. Choosing the right platforms like Amazon and optimizing your listings for SEO were crucial to your visibility and sales.

3. Scaling and Growth: As time progresses, you've learned how to manage inventory, optimize logistics, and use targeted marketing to scale the business. The implementation of new technologies and the expansion to international markets were milestones on your way.

4. Technological innovations and future trends**: You have realized that e-commerce is dynamic and constantly evolving. Integrating technologies like blockchain, big data, and AI not only opens up new opportunities, but also ensures you stay competitive.

5. Sustainability and ethical e-commerce**: In a world that increasingly values sustainability, you've understood the importance of implementing eco-friendly practices and maintaining transparent communication with your customers.

Looking to the future

The future of e-commerce continues to promise exciting developments. You are ready to meet these challenges with a clear view and an agile business strategy. The lessons from this guide will help you adapt to new technologies, adapt to changing market conditions, and continuously expand your vision.

Closing remarks

This trip was not only a professional experience, but also a personal journey of discovery. However, with passion, determination and a clear vision, anything is possible. May this guide continue to inspire you to pursue your dreams and boldly break new ground.

I wish you all the best on your future path in e-commerce and beyond. May your business continue to grow and flourish while enjoying a fulfilling life that harmoniously combines family and professional passion.

My request to you

First of all, I would like to thank you once again for buying this book about entrepreneurship, e-commerce and my career. It definitely shows me that you may have been in a similar situation to me right now and you just want more in your life. And that's a very important step to admit to yourself that you want to change something. As described at the beginning, write down what your motivation is to want to change something. Is it something material? That is, do you just want to be able to allow yourself more in your life? Or is it the social drive, i.e. maybe you want to give something back to your fellow human beings, the environment or people who may not be doing so well.

No matter what your motivation is, write it down and place it in such a way that you can look at it even in bad times and you know again why you are doing all this.

I wish you all the best and much success on this path. Don't let it get you down and look for people who also want to do more with your life, because in a group it is much easier and the exchange is much easier and is also strongly supportive of your business idea.

Don't let yourself be unsettled by others who may not believe in you and your idea. Always ask yourself, what allows him to say this that you can't? Has he perhaps failed himself before? Doesn't he want you to be more successful than him? Most of the time, these people are dissatisfied with their lives themselves and actually want to change something themselves, but don't know how.

Set big goals with several smaller milestones so that you will be rewarded again and again when you reach your goals. These can be material things or even nice vacations with your girlfriend, boyfriend or family. Please note that this book is not intended to advise on any tax or legal topics, so I definitely recommend that you go to an expert. I also can't give you any investment tips here, here I just want to show you the possibilities you have to increase your assets. Of course, there are also fluctuations here, so I can only recommend you to see an investment advisor. It is only intended to serve as motivation. Of course, it also does not guarantee you success, it is only intended to give you important tips so that you and your company can be on the best way there.

I still have a little something for you

Since you've read this far, I notice that you're really interested in the topic of business building, e-commerce and mindset.

If you want to see and learn more about these topics, then feel free to follow me on my social networks. Are you ready to get started and are just looking for the last few ideas or need support with marketing, construction, etc.? Feel free to write me a message on Instagram.

I really wish you all the best for the future and look forward to your message. Because one thing is certain. The best time to start was yesterday. You missed it? Anyway, just start today and set the first milestone in your life.

Best regards

Your Joshua

Instagram: @baumino.official

www.ingramcontent.com/pod-product-compliance
Lightning Source LLC
Chambersburg PA
CBHW071838210526
45479CB00001B/190